A Special Gift

Presented to:

....

From:

....

Date:

....

stories, sayings, and scriptures to Encourage and Inspire

hugs™

for
Grandparents

Stories by
DR. LARRY KEEFAUVER

Personalized Scriptures by
LEANN WEISS

HOWARD
PUBLISHING CO.
West Monroe, Louisiana

Our purpose at Howard Publishing is to:

- *Increase faith* in the hearts of growing Christians
- *Inspire holiness* in the lives of believers
- *Instill hope* in the hearts of struggling people everywhere

Because He's coming again!

Hugs™ for Grandparents © 1998 by Dr. Larry Keefauver
All rights reserved. Printed in the United States of America

Published by Howard Publishing Co., Inc.,
3117 North 7th Street, West Monroe, LA 71291-2227

01 02 03 04 05 06 07   10

Scriptures paraphrased by LeAnn Weiss, owner of Encouragement
Company, Orlando, Florida

Interior Design by LinDee Loveland
Edited by Janet Reed

Library of Congress Cataloging-in-Publication Data

Keefauver, Larry.
    Hugs for Grandparents : stories, sayings, and scriptures to encourage
and inspire / Larry Keefauver.
        p. cm.
    ISBN 1-878990-80-2
    1. Grandparents—Religious life. 2. Grandparenting—Religious
aspects —Christianity. I. Title.
BV4528.5.K44 1998
248.8'5—dc21   97-39215

"The Ten Commandments of Grandparenting" from GRANDCHIL-
DREN ARE SO MUCH FUN, I SHOULD HAVE HAD THEM FIRST
by Lois Wyse Copyright (c) 1992 by Lilla Rogers. Reprinted by permission
of Crown Publishers, Inc.

Contents

I give glory to God for my grandparents

and dedicate this book to them –

Leslie and Nell Quinn

Dewey and Irene Keefauver

The Ten Commandments of Grandparenting

1. Thou shalt not freak out when thy grandchild, to whom thou has just given a one-half interest in Mt. Rushmore plus two Oreo cookies, refuses to speak to thee on the telephone.

2. Thou shalt permit thy grandchildren to have other grandparents before thee on certain holidays.

3. Thou shalt honor the father and mother of thy grandchildren and thou shalt not substitute thy judgment for theirs.

4. Thou shalt open the doors of thy home and thy heart to thy grandchildren without screaming, "Don't touch," for thou knowest that the visit of thy grandchildren shall soon end.

5. Thou shalt remember thy family history and teach it diligently unto thy grandchildren.

6. Thou shalt refrain from exalting the roles of thy grandchildren, remembering always that thy friends also have grandchildren.

7. Thou shalt not commit effrontery; thou shalt answer the questions of thy grandchildren with dignity and respect.

8. Thou shalt not steal thy grandchild's witticism and pass it as thine own.

9. Thou shalt not covet thy neighbor's grandchild for his or her good grades, sweet disposition, or gentle manner.

10. Thou shalt love thy half-grandchildren, thy step-grandchildren, thy somewhat grandchildren as surely as thou lovest thy natural grandchildren, for it is the heart not the bloodline that truly makes thee a grandparent.

1

preserving innocence

Impressionable eyes are watching. Share the gift of the word of life I've placed in you. I've destined you to shine like the stars of the universe to those around you. Shine brightly in this crooked and depraved generation.

Love,
Your Father of Light

Philippians 2:14–16

As a grandparent, you can give the gift of wonder better than most. Why? Because you've seen enough of life's paradoxes and mysteries to understand that many questions don't have answers . . . and don't need them.

Trying to explain the inexplicable is the blight of a rational culture that has lost its sense of awe. Grandparents know that gazing at the stars and wondering what's out there is an activity worth sharing. Grandparents and grandchildren can share the wonder of a newborn baby, a field of wildflowers, a spider's web, or a soap bubble.

Part of the innocence of childhood is the ability to marvel at God's creation and all of its creatures, including ourselves. One of the greatest gifts a grandparent can give upcoming generations is a wide-eyed gaze that marvels at sunsets and sunrises, caterpillars and butterflies, falling stars and autumn moons.

As a grandparent, you can help preserve the innocence of your grandchildren – but there is a cost. You will have to give up any shreds of cynicism that may have crept into your heart, and you will need to open your eyes to the world of wonder as seen through the innocence of childlike faith.

Maintain your sense of awe. Gaze often at sunrises and sunsets. Meditate frequently on God's majesty. Grasp the wonder of creation and share your awe for an awesome God with your grandchildren.

If a child is to keep alive his inborn sense of wonder, he needs the companionship of at least one adult who can share it, rediscovering with him the joy, excitement and mystery of the world we live in.

—Rachel Carson

*For one more year, a child's innocence
had been preserved against the
onslaught of a cynical world.*

Grandma's wisdom

Each Christmas my grandparents came from Tennessee to celebrate the holidays with us. No one could cook like Grandmother. I loved sitting in the kitchen and talking with her as she baked all of her favorite holiday recipes – especially the Christmas cookies. If I was really good, she'd let me stir the cookie dough and lick the spoon. I will never forget the wonderful aromas and wisdom-filled talks we shared.

When I was old enough to go to school, I met new friends who seemed to know things far beyond anything ever revealed by my parents. One boy told me where babies came from, but his story sounded a little fishy. Why would storks go to all that trouble? A girl revealed to me why boys and girls were different: She secretly whispered that we were different so that girls could wear dresses – but boys had to wear pants. Gosh, I never wanted to wear a dress anyway!

But the most disturbing revelation of all came from my best friend, Buddy – and Buddy never lied to me. Buddy told me that there was no such person as Santa Claus. I couldn't believe it. Every year Santa had come faithfully to our house on Christmas Eve, leaving me great presents and eating the cookies and drinking the milk I left by the tree.

But Buddy told me that Santa was really my parents. I was shaken to the core. What a terrible Christmas it would be if Santa were really Mom and Dad! So one day after school, as I sat in the kitchen helping Grandmother bake cookies, I got up the nerve to ask her. I knew she wouldn't lie, and she seemed so old and wise that surely she knew everything – especially about Santa Claus.

"Grandmom, will you tell me the truth if I ask you something?" I ventured.

⌣ *Grandma's wisdom* ⌣

"If I know the answer, I will," she replied as she handed me a spoon filled with sugar cookie dough to lick clean.

"Well, my friend Buddy told me that there is no real Santa Claus. He said Santa is just Mom and Dad. Is that true?" I asked, holding my breath for the answer.

"Hmmm." She paused as she wiped her flour-covered hands on her handmade apron, which was brightly decorated with Christmas trees, stars, presents, and bears – she loved teddy bears. "I can't answer for sure. I'm really not an expert on Santa Claus. But I suggest that we just wait and see what happens this year. Watch your parents closely; never let them out of your sight. And if presents do appear under the tree and you don't see your parents put them there, then Santa must be real for you." Her eyes seemed to have an unusually bright twinkle in them as she turned back toward the oven to take out the next batch of cookies.

Her plan made perfect sense. I plotted to stay up all night on Christmas Eve and watch the tree from the crack under my bedroom door. I had a direct line of vision from my room, and I knew how I could make myself stay awake – I would drink lots of Coke.

∿ preserving innocence ∿

Every Christmas Eve our family went to a candlelight service at church that ended at midnight. My grandparents never went with us because it was too late for them; they always retired around 10:00 each evening. As usual, the service was beautiful, but all I could think about was staying awake. I had hidden a few bottles of Coke under my bed to help me. I prayed really hard that God would help me too.

That Christmas I was hoping to get a new bike. I knew my chances were slim, but I still held out hope. Since I had been really good, I felt that just maybe Santa would grant my request.

Walking in the front door at 12:30 A.M. on Christmas Day, I had one thought in mind: Go directly to my room and drink a Coke in order to stay awake. As I walked past the Christmas tree, a quick glance out of the side of my eye brought me to a screeching halt. There, in front of the tree, was the most beautiful red Flyer bike I had ever seen. I was stunned. Apparently, Santa had come while I was at church with my family. I checked the cookies and milk, and sure enough – all that was left of the cookies was a few crumbs, and the milk glass was empty.

⊹ Grandma's wisdom ⊱

I couldn't believe it. All my doubts about Santa vanished. My bike had training wheels, so I just sat on it for a while, dreaming about riding it down our street in just a few hours. I wanted so badly to tell my grandparents, but Mom insisted I not bother them since they were asleep. In ecstasy, I slipped into bed and said my prayers, remembering to thank God for Santa Claus and my new Ryder bike.

The next morning, I proudly showed my new bike to my grandparents, and I noticed that bright twinkle in Grandmom's eye again. As our Christmas tradition dictated, we gathered around the living room and read the story of Christ's birth from the book of Luke. Then each of us shared something we were thankful for: Mom and Dad expressed gratitude to God for blessing them with children; Grandmom and Grandfather thanked God for seeing their grandchildren filled with joy; and me, I just praised God for Santa and my new bike. Gently, Grandmom added, "Remember, the joy of Jesus' birth is a much greater joy than any present you will ever get under the tree."

So, for one more year, a child's innocence had been preserved against the onslaught of a cynical world. True, such a trivial thing means little in the annals of history, but it meant everything to me that night. As a teenager, I finally learned the truth. While the family was away at church, Grandfather had assembled my bike while Grandmom had looked on approvingly, eating cookies and sipping milk. And a few hours later, they sat peering through the crack beneath their bedroom door to witness the surprise and joy of their grandson.

I was shocked that my perfect, God-fearing grandparents had planned and pulled off such a deceitful conspiracy. Yet my shock was only momentary. I recognized their deep love in their desire to see me experience wonder and joy at Christmas. And I had matured to the point of understanding that the gift of God's love in Jesus truly was the greatest gift of all. And that gift was reflected ever so brightly in Grandmom and Grandfather.

reflections . . .

2

being there

I know about being there. When you've passed through trials, I've always been right there. I haven't let the storms of life overwhelm or drown you. I've protected you from the burn of the flames.

Love,
God, Your Ever Present Help
in Times of Trouble

Isaiah 43:2; Psalm 46:1

Comfort is like a favorite blanket on a cold night. It surrounds and warms us emotionally while protecting us from the chill of loss, grief, disappointment, and hurt.

Through years of life's ups and downs, grandparents have drawn upon God's *being there* in mercy and comfort to help them make it through the tough spots. They have discovered that when they need hope, God provides glimpses of assurance; when they need strength, God fills them with his own; and when they need a person to come near and help, the family of God is there for them, sharing God's tender words, reassuring hope, and unfailing love.

Grandparents are repositories of compassion. When a young, inexperienced traveler on life's highway breaks down, grandfather or grandmother can *be there* with a practical word of advice, a supportive listening ear, and a look or hug that says, *God and I are here to comfort and help you make it through.*

As life's seasons change, grandparents decide whether to become critics or comforters, takers or givers, escapers or encouragers.

Being there for a grandchild means holding him close during a frightening thunderstorm, helping her with the down payment on her first car, attending his ball games, listening to her poetry, wiping away his tears when a pet dies, and encouraging her when she embarrasses herself.

The choice to become a river of God's comfort, rather than a reservoir, releases into a new generation one of the lessons that grandparents teach best: *Just as I am here for you, your heavenly Father can be counted on to be with you always.*

21

When doubts filled my mind, your comfort gave me renewed hope.

—King David

*Then tragedy struck. Bud got loose from the house,
ran out into the road, and was hit by a car.
Thank God, Gramps was there.*

burying Bud

My grandparents were "snowbirds." Every winter they would join the many other snowbirds who flocked to Florida to enjoy the warm weather. As convenience would have it, my family lived in south Florida, so Gramps and Grandmom built a small, winter home right across the street from us in rural Broward County. And this is where they lived from Thanksgiving through Easter each year.

Every afternoon, Gramps picked me up from school and spent time with me until Mom got home from work. One of my after-school chores was walking and feeding

ᵜ being there ᵜ

our black cocker spaniel, Inky; so every afternoon, Gramps and I would walk the dog together.

Those were great excursions. We talked about everything. Believing my grandfather was one of the oldest and wisest men alive, I asked him all sorts of questions. My favorites were:

> How many stars are there in the universe?
> Why do dogs bite?
> How deep is the deepest part of the ocean?
> Since the canal along our property eventually flows into the ocean, could sharks swim into it and bite us if we swam in it?
> Why do we walk dogs but not cats?

One of my grandfather's favorite answers was, "Only God knows." For a long time I thought he was just trying to avoid giving me an answer, but years later I realized his wisdom. It's true – some things only God knows!

One afternoon when we arrived home after school, Mom was already there. She had tears in her eyes and a tiny, blond cocker spaniel in her arms.

∽ burying Bud ∾

"Mom, what's wrong? Where's Inky? Where did you get that puppy?" My rapid-fire questions exploded like firecrackers on the fourth of July.

"Right after you left for school this morning, Inky died. I knew you would be so sad and upset, so I stayed home from work, and Gramps and I went to the pet store to find a new dog for you," Mom explained. "His name is Bud."

Mom and Gramps were very wise. I did feel a twinge of grief for Inky, but Bud was so endearing that my attention immediately focused on the new puppy. The next few days were filled with the usual new-puppy chores of feeding, bathing, cleaning up messes, and trying to train Bud to walk on a leash.

Then tragedy struck. Bud got loose from the house, ran out into the road, and was hit by a car. Thank God, Gramps was there. Somehow, he *always* seemed to be there for me – just at the right time, just when I needed him most. He and I saw the accident together. As a ten-year-old, my life was shattered that day. It was hard to comprehend that first Inky and now Bud were dead. Grief stricken, I held my dead puppy close until Gramps finally pried him out of my arms and took him away to bury him.

I barely slept that night. The few times I did manage to drift off, my sleep was filled with nightmares, as I relived the accident over and over again. I could not believe Bud was dead. As soon as the sun rose, I slipped out of bed and crept over to Gramps's house. I found the shovel he had used to bury Bud still propped against the side of the house. I went into Gramps's backyard and looked for where he might have buried Bud the night before.

When I saw a patch of loose dirt, I started digging. After a few shovelfuls of dirt, I spotted another plot of loose dirt and began digging there, and then another and another. As hard as I tried, I could not find Bud's grave. I had dug about fifteen holes in the backyard before he woke up and came outside to see what I was doing.

"Son," he urged, "you must give up trying to find Bud. He's gone. Even if you found him, you could not bring your puppy back to life."

"But Gramps," I cried, "I must find him. I never really said good-bye. And if I pray for him, maybe God will raise him up to life. You know, like those people you read to me about from my Bible."

He smiled and took me into his arms. Then with a knowing look, he walked me over to a spot of freshly turned soil that I had missed. "This is the place," he said. I reached for the shovel to start digging for Bud, but he would not let me have the spade.

"Let him be," counseled my grandfather. Tears burned my eyes, and sobs began to erupt from my throat.

"But Gramps, we didn't even give him a funeral."

Then he disappeared into the house. He returned a few moments later with a Bible is his hand. Together, grandfather and grandson, we stood over Bud's grave, read a Scripture, prayed the Lord's Prayer, and said farewell to Bud. Then Gramps held me close, and we cried together.

Of all the meaningful times I had with my grandfather, I remember this time most. I suppose the pain a grandfather shares with you means more than the laughter or fun. As we walked into the house, I asked Gramps another one of my questions, "Gramps, are there dogs in heaven?"

"Only God knows," he replied, and I knew that Gramps must be the wisest man alive.

reflections...

31

3

pass it on

I have blessed you! Pass on your sincere faith from generation to generation. Fan into flame my unique gift which is in you.

Love,
Your God of Marvelous Works and Deeds

2 Timothy 1:5

Grandparents have incredible wisdom to share with their grandchildren, for they have seen God's truths at work for decades. A lifetime of putting God's truths into practice results in sterling wisdom.

Each precious, God-given lesson can become a jewel to be grasped and treasured by grandchildren. Don't waste your laughter or your tears; share their wisdom with your grandchildren.

Wisdom is the gold mined from the ore of difficulties and refined in the fires of patience, practice, and prayer. Grandchildren can discover through the instruction of their grandparents that wisdom is *God's best, done God's way, in God's time.*

Your wisdom, remembered by your grandchildren, will serve as a voice of guidance and direction through difficult decisions and tough trials. Anchor your wisdom in God's so that the voice they hear through yours is *his!*

Pass it on – pass the wisdom God has given you to your grandchildren. When all other gifts break, wear out, or become obsolete, wisdom endures the test of time and gives future generations an eternal perspective.

I think with you,

that nothing is of

more importance for

the public weal, than

to form and train up

youth in wisdom and

virtue.

—*Ben Franklin*

Pops and his grandson talked about things
that Peter had never shared with me.
I suppose it's safer to talk about certain
things with a grandfather.

fishing

As a boy, my main recreation with Dad was fishing. Two or three Saturdays each month, we got up about two hours before sunrise. Dad always cooked our standard breakfast – two eggs, bacon, and toast. I would swallow breakfast whole in anticipation of heading to the Everglades and all the bass we would catch.

Then when my son, Peter, was old enough, Dad (Pops), Peter, and I went fishing together. Peter would be just as excited as I had been. Only now, when we got up two hours before dawn, we stopped at a pancake house on the way out to the canal.

Pops was much more patient with Peter than he had ever been with me. I reckon that by the time you're a grandfather, you have mellowed some and learned more patience. Peter would repeatedly get lures snagged in the weeds or hung up on tree branches and Pops would never yell or raise his voice – like he had at me.

I enjoyed watching Pops teach his grandson how to fish. With each cast, Peter improved as Pops encouraged him. We shared all kinds of fish lore as Pops told Peter about the biggest bass he had ever caught – and the ones that got away.

More important, Pops and his grandson talked about things that Peter had never shared with me. I suppose it's safer to talk about certain things with a grandfather. I stayed very quiet in the boat just observing and listening. Miraculously, Peter seemed to forget I was there. Like a parent chauffeuring young teens and overhearing things they would never share directly, I was there at several sacred moments. I even relished the fishing conversation between grandfather and grandson.

Pops, what makes the fish bite?

How do you know where the fish are?

❖ fishing ❖

When will a big bass strike?

How come they hit a lure when it's not alive?

Where do bass live?

Why do you have to get up so early to go fishing?

Do bass only bite early in the morning? Do they
ever sleep in?

And so the questions continued. Pops always had an answer. His answers never made scientific sense, but that didn't seem to bother Peter. He knew he had Pops's undivided attention, and he basked in the glory of that.

Just as he had with me, Pops used fishing to teach Peter some important lessons in life. The first was patience. Sometimes we would fish for hours without even so much as a nibble. Whenever Peter became fidgety, Pops would simply say, "Patience, Son, have patience. You never accomplish anything in life without patience."

Peter often protested that going fishing was a waste of time if we didn't catch anything. His grandfather just used Peter's complaints as another teaching moment. "Just being in God's outdoors is enough, Son. Just being out here is more important than catching anything," Pops would say.

✌ pass it on ✎

The place we fished always had alligators. In fact, the canals we fished in ran parallel to a road named Alligator Alley. Peter was fascinated by the alligators floating lazily in the water, sunning themselves on a hot, humid day. "If I fell in, would they bite me?" Peter would ask.

Pops always answered, "If you leave them alone, they'll leave you alone. Mind your own business, and they'll mind theirs." He would then proceed to lecture Peter on the virtues of not being nosey. With his dark brown eyes fixed on Pops, Peter took in every word, as he pondered Pops's advice.

Peter still talks about some of Pops's sayings. Though more than a decade has passed since our fishing trips, Peter remembers the wisdom Pops shared during those special times. Perhaps the most memorable bit of wisdom came the day Peter's open-faced spinning reel got a loop in it. Peter ignored the loop and cast his lure anyway, throwing his line into a terrible knot.

Pops told him to unravel the knot, and Peter worked quite some time trying to disentangle his line. Finally, on the verge of tears, Peter threw his pole down in frustration and announced that the knot was impossible to untie.

⌒: fishing :⌒

Without saying a word, Pops picked up the line, cut the knot out of it, and rewound Peter's reel.

"Why did you do that?" Peter asked. "You wasted all that line."

Pops nodded as he cast the lure out for Peter and got him fishing again. "We didn't come here to untie knots," Pops said somewhat sternly. "We came here to fish. You can't catch fish if you spend all your time getting knots out of your line." Peter nodded and soon afterward caught a fish. I thought about the wisdom of Pops's statement. So many people spend too much time working on their equipment, getting ready for life, while much of real life passes them by. As I watched grandfather and grandson fish together, I realized that they were really *living life* in those precious moments. Instead of just getting ready, Pops spent his time actually fishing.

As grandparents, all the plans and dreams we have for our grandchildren will never make a difference unless we actually spend time with them. There comes the critical time when we must stop fixing our tackle and begin fishing. Are you fishing yet?

reflections . . .

4

saying
good-bye

My precious, righteous child, remember my promise for you. The righteous will flourish like a palm tree. You'll grow like a cedar of Lebanon. I will transplant you into my own garden under my personal care. You will flourish and thrive in my courts. Even in your old age, you will keep bearing fruit. I will preserve you and keep your life growing fresh, vibrant, and vital.

Love,

Your Father of Life

Psalm 92:12–14

Grandchildren do not remember their grandparents for how they began their race. Obviously, they weren't there. Rather, they remember their grandparents for how they finished. After years of raising a family, working hard, worshiping God, and serving others, a grandparent in the latter years of life makes a final statement. This final statement is like a book's conclusion, like a race's finish line, a game's score, or a friend's eulogy.

It's not how fast or strong you start that counts – it's how you finish.

This is not a season for withdrawing and putting up your feet. Living life only to retire and do nothing is such a waste. As work responsibilities decrease, time that was invested in making a living can now be invested in lives, particularly the lives of "the least of these" – the sick, the helpless, the imprisoned, the lonely, the poor, and the children, especially grandchildren. Are you managing your people investments as well as your financial ones?

Investing yourself in loving and serving others fulfills Jesus' revelation, *He that would be great among you must be servant of all.* Before saying good-bye, break life's winner's tape by finishing strong!

In the Christian life it's not how you start; it's how you finish. . . . Go and finish strong for Christ!

—Tommy Barnett

"God loves you and so do I," Pop whispered with an effort-filled breath. Missy lifted his hand to her lips and blew a kiss for him.

Pop's farewell

Pop was the reigning patriarch of a clan that spanned four generations. For decades he had planned the family reunions, bailed the grandchildren and their children out of financial messes, and offered counsel on everything from mending marriages to disciplining kids to buying a first home. As busy as he had been with his business – working in his retail store until cancer struck him at seventy – Pop had made time for his children's families, including the great-grandchild who had just celebrated her fourth birthday.

ᴥ saying good-bye ᴥ

But cancer had taken its toll, and in the last few months, Pop's always bronzed skin had turned ashen as he had wasted away from a trim, fit 170 pounds to a wispy 110. Always decisive, he had rejected the arduous radiation and chemotherapy treatments that might have prolonged his life for six months and had chosen instead a hospice program that allowed him to manage his pain and stay at home. His days at home had been especially brightened by constant visits from his great-granddaughter, Missy.

Though fully alert, Pop was dying. His blood pressure was falling, and his breathing was becoming increasingly labored. The family was gathering for his final hours. Propped up in his favorite chair, he weakly greeted and smiled at the children and grandchildren as they came into the family room to be with him. Everyone understood how weak Pop was except Missy. With bouncing, auburn curls and deep brown eyes, she had come to believe that Pop was her very own. Each day for months she had visited him, bringing bouquets of wildflowers, special stones and colored rocks, and her favorite book – *Curious George.* In fact, she carried a stuffed Curious George and the book everywhere she went.

∿ Pop's farewell ∿

On this final day of life for Pop, Missy came bounding into the family room, which was shrouded in somberness. Not noticing anyone else, Missy darted across the room and carefully climbed into the chair next to Pop. Putting Curious George on Pop's lap, she opened up her book and enthusiastically asked, "Pop, read me about George."

Eyes brimming with tears and love, Pop mustered his strength and faintly whispered, "Pop is too tired today, honey."

"Then I'll read it to you," she replied, not missing a beat.

"Not now, Missy. I'm getting ready to go on a trip," whispered Pop.

Immediately, Missy closed the book and picked up on her favorite topic – trips. She loved to ride in the car, and she continually asked her parents when they would take her on the next camping trip.

"Can I go with you, Pop? Can we go camping together?"

Pop's tears became a steady stream. In fact, among the assembled family, not a dry eye could be found. Silently, all the children and grandchildren moved closer to hear the duo's conversation.

"You can't come on this trip. I'll be gone a long time. But someday, you will come see me," Pop explained as Missy took Curious George's hands and wiped the tears from Pop's cheeks.

For a few moments Missy was silent. Many in the room had almost stopped breathing. Between the reality that these were Pop's last few hours and the poignancy of the conversation, the rest of the family realized that Missy was God's special ambassador to bring out Pop's final good-bye.

Missy reached out and gently took Pop's face into her hands, pulling him so close to her face that their noses almost touched.

"Pop," she whispered knowingly, "is your trip gonna be to heaven? 'Cause if it is, I know all about it there. Mom told me that it's beautiful and that nobody is sick there. I don't want you to be sick anymore, Pop. 'Member how we used to play tag in the backyard? You and me and George. Can we do that again when I come visit you?"

༄ Pop's farewell ༄

"Yes, honey, anything you want," Pop barely whispered. Missy then kissed Pop good-bye. He closed his eyes for a moment, gathering his last few ounces of strength. All the children and grandchildren closed in around Pop and Missy and reached out to touch them, forming a prayer circle. Pop slowly opened his eyes, glistening with tears, and looked at each person in the room.

"Pop, do that prayer you always say to everybody before we go home," Missy asked. "And then blow me a kiss, okay?"

"God loves you and so do I," Pop whispered with an effort-filled breath. Missy lifted his hand to her lips and blew a kiss for him. Each child and grandchild blew him a kiss, as had been done for so many years, and echoed, "Pop, God loves you and so do I."

The blessing had been given. The final good-bye had been said and anointed with tears. Pop closed his eyes and began the trip he had prepared a lifetime to take.

reflections . . .

5

I

inspiring
God ideas

Point your loved ones to aim for the crown that will last forever! Don't let them run aimlessly or get disqualified for the prize. Challenge them to serve God's unique purpose for them in their own generation.

Love always,
Jesus

1 Corinthians 9:24–27

Simply stated, there are only two kinds of ideas: bad ideas and God ideas. *But wait,* you may protest. What about good ideas? In the Garden of Eden, there were only two trees: the Tree of Life and the Tree of the Knowledge of Good and Evil. Good ideas are merely bad ideas with a sugar-coating. Good ideas are described in proverbial wisdom as ways that seem right to humans but end in death! Anything that's not a God idea falls short of his grace, glory, and purposes.

When a God idea is birthed by God's Spirit within the heart and mind of a grandchild, a grandparent has a solemn, sacred duty to do everything possible to fan that smoldering coal into a blazing fire of zeal, passion, and action. Like the bellows of an ironsmith's furnace breathing hot the fire that refines metal, so a grandparent's breath of encouragement for a

grandchild transforms a Spirit-breathed
God idea into a fiery flame that ignites hope
and possibilities within a child.

The enemy comes to rob, steal, and destroy
God ideas. But no enemy can cut through the
hedge of protection planted around a grandchild by
a grandparent's prayers and positive support.

So what is a God idea? Whenever a grandchild
wants to love instead of hate, hug instead of crush,
give instead of take, serve instead of be served, or
heal instead of hurt, such ideas come right from
the throne of God into the heart of that child.
So be the wind of encouragement for every
God idea planted in your grandchild.
When you affirm God ideas, you will
see miracles surround your grandchild . . . and you!

There is a God thought for you! God has a God idea for each step we take. Good ideas may come to pass, but God ideas must come to pass.

—Tim Storey

*Isn't it wonderful that grandparents are there
to help the God ideas inspired within
their grandchildren become realities?*

Thanksgiving and a God idea

Each Thanksgiving during his childhood, a friend of mine visited his grandparents who lived right outside of Philadelphia. As a small child, he loved to travel by the trolley cars and subway into downtown Philadelphia to see the awesome decorations and window displays in the stores.

One Thanksgiving when Tom was eleven years old, a big snowstorm hit the city, and it was freezing cold. His grandfather didn't want to take the traditional pilgrimage into the city on the Friday after Thanksgiving, but Tom insisted.

⌇ inspiring God ideas ⌇

After consulting the outside thermometer and listening to the weather report, his grandfather decided that he could tolerate the visit to the inner city. As always, Tom enjoyed the ride on the trolleys and subway. It was an exciting adventure filled with unusual sounds, smells, sights, and people.

As grandfather and grandson emerged from Penn Station, they saw piles of snow and snowplows working hard to clear the city streets. Most of the sidewalks were passable, and the two made their way toward Market Street and their favorite store of all, Wanamakers, which was always fabulously decorated for the holiday season.

Suddenly, Tom stopped in his tracks. Surprised, his grandfather asked, "What's the holdup, Tom? We're almost at Wanamakers."

For a few moments Tom just stared at the city sight in front him. It was the first time he had ever seen a homeless person sleeping on a subway grate for its warm air. Curled up in a ball and covered with newspapers, this transient slept soundly, warmed by the updrafts rising from the subway tunnels below.

"Grandpa, he doesn't have a blanket," protested Tom.

◦ᘓ Thanksgiving and a God idea ᘓ◦

"Yes, I know," replied Grandpa. He took Tom's hand and pulled him from the all too common street scene and toward the bright lights and sounds of holiday cheer just around the corner.

Yet he noticed that his grandson did not seem to enjoy his tour through Wanamakers as he had in the past. A somber countenance had replaced his usual smile. Tom said very little as they retraced their steps to the subway that evening. He was deep in thought.

Arriving home, Tom excused himself from dinner, saying he wasn't hungry, and went immediately to his bedroom. His grandparents exchanged surprised looks. Thanksgiving leftovers of hot turkey sandwiches were one of Tom's favorite meals. They decided to leave him alone as he worked through his thoughts and feelings from the day.

Early the next morning, much to his grandparents's surprise, Tom was awake and sitting at the kitchen table before they rose.

"Grandpa, can we talk?" he queried.

"Of course," came the reply as Grandpa sat down at the table, coffee cup in hand. Grandmother listened to the conversation as she fixed Tom's favorite breakfast of biscuits and gravy.

"Grandpa, we have so much, and that man sleeping on the street has nothing," he proceeded.

"Yes, that's true," affirmed Grandpa.

"Couldn't we do something about that?" probed Tom.

"Perhaps," responded his grandfather. "What do you have in mind?"

"Do you and Grandmother have any extra blankets?" Tom asked.

"Yes, we might have some," answered Grandpa.

"Could we take them to the people sleeping on the grates? I believe that's what we should do if we are really thankful for all our blessings," said Tom.

Grandpa was somewhat surprised by Tom's proposal, but he was pleased nonetheless. He knew that this wasn't just a good idea, it was a God idea. And God ideas must be acted upon. He glanced over to see Grandmother's response, only to realize she had disappeared from the kitchen. She rejoined them a few moments later with four blankets stacked neatly in her arms.

Thanksgiving and a God idea

"I don't need these," she said to her grandson. "You and Grandpa take them to those needy and homeless people in the city," she instructed as tears welled up in her eyes.

"Grandpa, could I go around the neighborhood and collect some other blankets too? Maybe some of your friends would help out," Tom requested. Grandpa nodded, and together they spent the day going door to door collecting old blankets for the homeless.

Sunday morning was crisp and fresh with the sun shining brightly on the newly fallen snow. Grandpa and Tom piled Tom's old wagon high with blankets. It would be difficult to transport them, but somehow they would deliver their precious cargo to the street people that afternoon. Tom was so excited he could barely wait to bolt from the church to the car after the morning service.

Grandfather and grandson spent the afternoon sharing warmth with Philadelphia's homeless. Tom now says that was his most memorable and meaningful Thanksgiving ever. No turkey dinner, football game, or trip to Wanamakers could ever compare with the true reason for the season he discovered with his grandfather that Thanksgiving. Isn't it wonderful that grandparents are there to help the God ideas inspired within their grandchildren become realities?

reflections . . .

6

T
taking
time

Remember, this is not your home! Your life here is quickly passing by. Let me teach you to number your days. Ask me to show you how to spend them wisely. Then watch me give you a heart of wisdom.

Love,
Your God of All Wisdom

Psalm 90:10–11

Too busy! That has become the byword of our times. *Too busy* is our excuse for shallow relationships and lack of intimacy. But too busy doing what? Ah, now there's the key – doing instead of being.

Busyness is about doing, but grandparenting is about being. Being there for family. Being real, transparent, truthful, and open. Being like Jesus. Taking the time just to be there says more about love than anything we might do. Remember, taking time requires your presence.

Being a grandparent means taking time for the special moments in a grandchild's life; taking the time to listen, no matter how trivial the conversation; taking time to forgive in spite of the hurt; and allowing God's light to shine through you, no matter how dark life becomes.

Being a grandparent means praising instead of pushing, comforting instead of criticizing, giving instead of getting, and loving instead of lecturing.

By spending time with your grandchildren you give them a "savings bond" that earns eternal interest. What does time buy that money cannot? Friendship, fellowship, sharing, trust, understanding, and intimacy.

Taking time for your grandchildren will fill your days with joy and lasting significance.

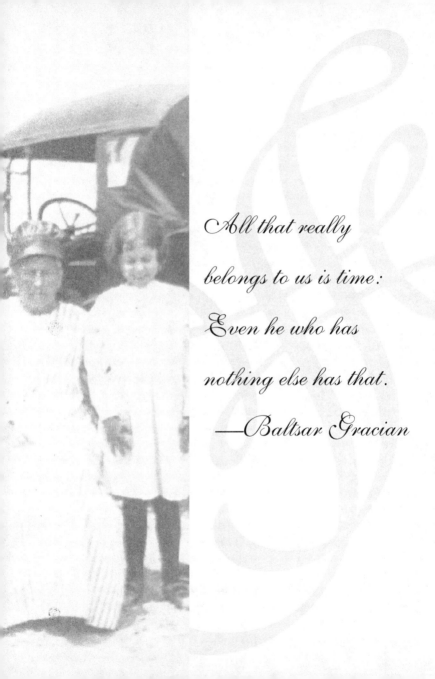

All that really belongs to us is time: Even he who has nothing else has that.

—Baltsar Gracian

*True, I had no time. True, I couldn't make all the
practices and games. But I was the greatest —
the greatest grandfather around.*

too old and too busy to coach

I gazed into the mirror and pondered the recent turn of events. I was not yet fifty, and not only did I have three grandchildren, but I also had full responsibility for fathering them. Their own father had left. What I had expected to be the freedom years of my life as an empty nester were busier than ever with work, grandparenting, and trying to juggle too many plates at once.

A person can do a lot of thinking while shaving, and as I slid the razor down my face, my mind wandered to all the reasons I didn't have the time or the energy to coach

⤳ taking time ⤫

Billy's Little League team. Billy is my ten-year-old grandson. He's a great kid, but this coaching thing could be the straw that would break the proverbial camel's back.

First, there is my job. I travel a four-state region as a manufacturer's rep. Some weeks I leave on Monday and don't return until Friday. I would have to miss a considerable number of Billy's practices. Then there was church. I had just become chairman of the deacons. We had a ton of visits and calls to make each month, in addition to our meetings. Of course, there was also my wife, Becky. I had looked forward to doing more with her in these empty-nest years – more travel, more dates, more time together. Now my grandchildren threatened to rob me of that precious time.

I finished shaving with more than the usual number of nicks. I was upset. Grabbing my glove and a bag of bats and other equipment, I rushed to the car and made my way to Billy's house. As I drove, I practiced my excuses.

Billy, I can't coach your team. I will be out of town too much, and it wouldn't be fair to miss so many games.

~ too old and too busy to coach ~

Uh, Billy, don't you think Granddad is just a little too old to do this coaching thing? Why don't I just come to your games and practices when I can but not coach the team.

Billy, you know I'm not as young as I used to be. Wouldn't you rather have a younger coach, someone who can play baseball well? I'm really rusty.

I weighed my excuses and refined my words. Of course, no ten-year-old could stand up against the logic and authority of a grandfather. Besides, I could probably make it easier for him if I took him over to Sports Authority and bought him that new glove he had been drooling over for weeks. Yes! That's it. Excuses and bribery always work with grandchildren.

As I turned down his street, I saw Billy standing on the front walk just waiting for me. Uniform on . . . hat in place . . . bat and glove over his shoulder, Billy was intently staring down the road watching for my car. As soon as he spied me, he began waving and running toward me.

He rushed up to the car, threw open the door, and tumbled into the passenger seat. His stuff flew into the backseat with a practiced toss.

⌒∴ taking time ∴⌒

"Granddad, I thought you'd never get here. I can't wait for you to coach. Remember that pitch you taught me? I've been practicing it with Eric. Wait till you see it! It's awesome. I've told all the guys at school what a *killer coach* you're gonna be. Man, thanks for being our coach. You're the greatest."

Somehow . . . somewhere . . . all my excuses and bribes evaporated. True, I had no time. True, I couldn't make all the practices and games. So the other coach would just have to pick up the slack. But I was the greatest – the greatest grandfather around. And with God's help, I would step up to the plate of this new challenge and smack a home run. After all, my grandson would be around for a long time. He was worth all the time and effort I could manage to invest in him.

"Billy, I'm really looking forward to coaching. I hope it's okay if I miss a few games and practices with all my work travel," I explained.

"No sweat, Granddad. By the way, we're going right by Sports Authority on the way to the field. Can we stop and look one more time at that awesome glove?"

❧ too old and too busy to coach ❧

"Sure," I replied. I knew I was had! Billy would get his glove. It would be an outright gift, not a bribe. As for me, I got my gift as well — a grandson who believed in me. What more could a man want in his empty-nest years!

reflections . . .

7

lasting
truths

Remember what will last forever! The physical things you teach will have some value now, but godliness has value for all things, holding promise for both the present and the eternal. I've given you my God-breathed Word so that you may be fully equipped for every good work.

Love,
Your God of the Eternal Word

1 Timothy 4:8; 2 Timothy 3:16

The truths of Scripture are meant to be lived. But how? In order to be lived, truth must first be planted deep into our hearts. Then it can grow into actions, thoughts, and feelings. Truth grows as a vibrant tree from which others can pick and enjoy the good fruit of love, joy, peace, patience, faithfulness, kindness, humility, and self-discipline.

What kind of fruit will your life bear for the generations that follow you? Remember — judge and be judged, be critical and be criticized, put down others and they will put you down. But love and be loved, be merciful and receive mercy, give and it will be given to you in abundance.

We reap what we sow into the lives of our children and our children's children. The truth we sow is never just what we speak; it's also how we live. The fruit of your life will become painfully or joyfully evident in your grandchildren. Proverbs 13:22 reminds us that good grandparents leave an inheritance for their children's children. The life you live is the inheritance you leave. Live and leave lasting truths.

Absolute truth is

that which is true for

all people, for all

times, for all places.

—Josh McDowell

Grandmother would say, "Robert, your name is right here in the Bible." And then she would show me how she had crossed through "world" in John 3:16 and written my name in its place!

Grandmother's Bible

I am a preacher. In fact, I'm the first preacher ever in my family. I didn't intend to be a preacher; my original goal was to run for office and be elected to Congress. I guess you could say that my goal and God's plan led to different paths – until God spoke through Grandmother.

Every day after school when I came through the front door, Grandmother would be sitting there waiting for me. She came to live with us after Pops died. It worked out well for all of us. Grandmother didn't have to live alone, and she was always there for me after school while my parents were at work. She always had something ready for me to eat. I was usually starving after school. The cafeteria food was terrible, and besides, I often skipped lunch to save my lunch money for the next video game I wanted. My parents always seemed surprised when I had so much extra money for video games.

When I came home hungry, Grandmother saved the day. As I gulped down the sandwich she fixed, she would ask me about school, my friends, and my soccer team. We had great visits. So how did that lead to my being a preacher?

Well, after my snack, Grandmother always insisted we read a verse together from her Bible. It was very old and filled with her handwritten notes. She had kept a record of all the major points from every sermon, lesson, and Bible study she had heard. Grandmother's Bible was a full commentary.

Her favorite way to teach me a verse was to make it personal for me. *The Lord is Robert's shepherd, Robert shall not want.* Or, *For Robert is God's workmanship, created in Christ Jesus to do good works.* But my favorite verse was John 3:16, and she read it to me often. First, Grandmother would say, "Robert, your name is right here in the

Bible." And then she would show me how she had crossed through "world" and written my name in its place! I loved seeing my name in the Bible. I felt so important!

Then the day came when she read a verse from Romans. *How, then, shall they preach, except they be sent? And how shall they believe in him of whom they have not heard? And how shall they hear without Robert to tell them?*

In that moment, I didn't hear Grandmother's familiar voice. I heard from God. When you think about it, God really can speak through grandmothers and grandfathers if only they will let him. I know that he spoke to me through my grandmother that afternoon.

My grandfather had lots of old cigar boxes, and Grandmother would let me stack them one on top of the other to form a makeshift pulpit. I would borrow her Bible and preach a sermon. She listened intently and would always tell me how great my "sermon" was. I cannot remember one word of those bygone sermons, but I always see her smiling face when I stand before a real pulpit now.

Now I'm forty and Grandmother has been with Jesus for many years. After I preached her funeral, Dad gave me her Bible. That book, which I had seen for so many years opened on her lap, now lies open on my desk. Each week as I sit down to prepare a message, I use many resources, dictionaries, and commentaries. But I'm never fully ready to preach until I have consulted Grandmother's Bible. In a real way, she's still teaching me God's Word after all these years.